Maldon

Also by Michael Smith (* indicates a Shearsman publication)

POETRY
With the Woodnymphs
Times and Locations
Familiar Anecdotes
Stopping to Take Notes
Selected Poems
Lost Genealogies & Other Poems
Meditations on Metaphors
The Purpose of the Gift. Selected Poems*
Collected Poems*
Prayers for the Dead*

TRANSLATIONS
Federico García Lorca: *The Tamarit Poems*
Luis de Góngora: *Selected Shorter Poems*
Miguel Hernández: *Unceasing Lightning*
Antonio Machado: *Early Poems*
Pablo Neruda: *Twenty Love Poems & a Poem of Despair*
Francisco de Quevedo: *On the Anvil*

Cantes flamencos / Flamenco Songs (with Luis Ingelmo) *
Maldon & Other Translations*
Poems from Other Tongues*
Gustavo Adolfo Bécquer: *Collected Poems / Rimas* (with Luis Ingelmo) *
Fernando de Herrera: *Selected Poems* (with Luis Ingelmo)*
Antonio Machado: *Solitudes & Other Early Poems* (with Luis Ingelmo)*
Aníbal Núñez: *Selected Poems* (with Luis Ingelmo)*
Claudio Rodríguez: *Collected Poems* (with Luis Ingelmo) *
César Vallejo: *The Complete Poems* (with Valentino Gianuzzi) *
Juan Antonio Villacañas: *Selected Poems* *
                     (with Luis Ingelmo & Beatriz Villacañas)
Verónica Volkow: *Arcana & Other Poems* (with Luis Ingelmo)*

As editor:
James Clarence Mangan: *Selected Poems*
Irish Poetry: The Thirties Generation

Michael Smith

Maldon

A Version

Shearsman Books

First separate publication, 2019, by
Shearsman Books Ltd.,
58 Velwell Road,
Exeter EX4 4LD

www.shearsman.com

Previously published as part of
Maldon & Other Poems,
by Michael Smith,
Shearsman Books & New Writers' Press, 2004.

ISBN 978-1-84861-653-0

Illustration on the front cover by Louis de Brocquy,
copyright © Louis de Brocquy, 2004.
Reproduced by permission of the artist.

Rear cover photograph of the author by Barbara Smith.

MALDON

A Version

Translator's Note

The battle described in this fragment of epic took place on 10 or 11 August 991, at Maldon on the River Blackwater (then called the Panta) in Essex.

A band of Vikings led by Justin and Guthmund made an incursion into the east coast of England. Having plundered Ipswich, they moved into Essex as far as Maldon. The river near this town divides into two branches. The southern branch washes the northern slope of the hill on which the town is situated. It is here that the Danish ships seem to have taken up their position. It is usually assumed that the Vikings were on Northey Island, having come upriver. The East-Saxon earl, Byrhtnoth, came down from the north with as many men as he could quickly muster and encamped on the mainland, opposite the causeway. It is on the shores of this river that the battle was fought.

It is not known who composed the verses of the fragment. Scholars are of the *opinion* that the surviving fragment constitutes as much as seventy five per cent of the original.

For its rhythm and other effects this version is heavily and shamelessly indebted to Ezra Pound ('The Seafarer') and Basil Bunting ('Briggflatts'). I found it impossible to avoid all archaisms of diction and syntax, try how I would. I can only hope that what remains of the archaic does not impede the splendid thrust and rush of the original, and that it may, in fact, contribute something to the retention of its ancient flavour. I have not attempted to replicate slavishly the original metre, which would doubtless result in literary taxidermy, but rather to suggest it, as the French poet and critic Yves Bonnefoy sagely advised modern translators of poetic texts of past times and cultures.

In the opening and closing of 'Maldon', I have consciously retained the fragmentary nature of the piece because I think it adds a sense of authenticity and realism. As regards the seemingly inconsequential detail of the young warrior releasing his hawk, I agree with the Argentinian writer, Jorge Luis Borges, who greatly liked the text, that 'Given the epic harshness of the poem, the phrase *lêofne ... hafoc* (literally, 'his beloved hawk') moves us extraordinarily' (*Dada la dureza épica del poema, la frase 'el querido halcón', nos conmueve singularmente*).

Many years ago when I was a student in University College, Dublin, I made a literal translation of 'The Battle of Maldon' as part of my studies at the time. Of all the Old English poems I struggled with, the two that impressed me most for their purely literary qualities were 'The Seafarer' and 'Maldon'. Pound had already definitively done 'The Seafarer' and that was that. But 'Maldon' had not been so well served so far as I knew, and I toyed with the idea of attempting a version myself. But I did not attempt a translation then. Recently, however, having discovered by chance and read again my old student crib, I was once more enthused by the text and thought I might attempt what I had not dared to do in the past. I can only hope that my temerity at this late date has been at least partially justified.

Finally, a comment might perhaps be made on an Irish poet translating what is, among other things, an English national text. The events described in 'The Battle of Maldon' might just as easily, with a change of names of persons and places, serve as a description of what took place at Dublin's Clontarf in 1014. Borges would assuredly appreciate this conjunction of circumstances. And on an even more personal note, I would like to thank my wife Irene and my friend and fellow poet, Trevor Joyce, for their encouragement and other helpful contributions in the making of this translation.

Michael Smith
Dublin, 2004

Acknowledgements

For scholarly assistance with my translation I am hugely indebted to Elisabeth Okasha of University College Cork, whose generosity with her time and energy saved me from many a pitfall; needless to say, however, she is not to be held responsible for any of my own shortcomings.

With equal generosity and rapidity, Louis le Brocquy responded to my request for a cover drawing. His enthusiastic reading of the text was a great encouragement to me.

Further Reading

B. Mitchell and F. C. Robinson, eds., *A Guide to Old English*, 5th ed. Oxford, 1992; see pages 241-52.

D. G. Scragg, ed., *The Battle of Maldon*, 1981, Manchester University Press.

E. Treharne, ed., *Old and Middle English: An Anthology*. Oxford 2000, Basil Blackwell; see pages 141-55.

J. Cooper, ed., *The Battle of Maldon: Fiction and Fact*. London, 1993. Hambledon.

                                      … it was sundered.

He said to his soldiers

                    to set free their horses,

to drive them far off,

                    and on foot to fare forth,

to think of their hands

                    and boldness of bravery.

Then the kinsman of Offa

                    first found out

that the earl was unwilling

                    to countenance cowardice.

From his hands he let fly

                    his falcon, his fair one,

toward the wood in the distance,

                    and he went to the battle.

Thereby one might know
                              that the youth was unwilling
to waver in combat
                    when weapons he wielded.

He also desired Ealdric
                            to attend to his leader,
his lord, in the battle;
                          then forward began to bear
spear to the conflict:
                        and he was of hale heart
while he could bear with his hands
                                      his buckler and broad-blade.
His pledge to his prince to fight
                                  he upheld as he promised.

Then Byrhtnoth began
                        to exhort his soldiers;
he rode and he heartened,
                            showed to his warriors
the way they must stand
                          and hold to their stances;
he bade them grip their shields
                                  correctly and strongly,
and be unafraid.

When these he'd well heartened
                                  then he dismounted
where those of his men,
                          his dearest, most loyal retainers,
the troop of his household,
                              he knew to be stationed.

There stood then on shore

     and shouted out stoutly

the Vikings' envoy;

    voiced in words

full of menace

   the message of the seafarers

addressed to the earl

    where he stood on the bank:

'To you the bold seamen

    have sent me,

commanded me tell you

    to render up tribute

in return for protection;

    and for you it is better

to buy off with tribute

    this onslaught of spears

than take part with us

    in a battle so bitter.

There's no need either

    for mutual slaughter

if you have riches enough

    and give up your gold

in trade for a truce.

    If you who are strongest

decide to disband

    and pay to the seamen

the gold they determine

    as tribute for peace,

we shall take to our ships

    with the coins you have yielded,

set forth on the sea

    and keep peace with you.'

Byrhtnoth then spoke;
                    he grasped his buckler,
brandished his trim spear of ash;
                            angry and resolute,
made answer
               as follows:
'Listen, seaman,
                to what this folk tell you.
For tribute they'll give you
                      lances and spears
tipped with poison,
                 and ancient swords.
Such war-gear to you
                will be useless in battle.
Viking seaman,
              announce back again,
report to your people
                 a message more hateful,
that here stands dauntless
                  an earl with his troops
prepared to defend
              this land that is theirs,
Aethelred's homeland,
              my prince,
its people and places.
                The heathen shall fall
prostrate in battle.
              To me it's too shameful
that you with our tribute
                 depart on your ships
untested by battle,
            having journeyed
thus hither
         far in our homeland.

Nor shall you so easily
                    carry off treasure:
point and edge
                    must decide for us
in fierce sport of battle
                    before we give tribute.'

He bade them bear bucklers,
                    the warriors to go forth,
those men on the bank-side
                    to hold to their stances.
Because of the water
                    no troops could engage.

There came then flowing
                    flood after ebb-tide,
tidal currents fused;
                    the time seemed lengthy
until all together
                    their spears they could bear.
They stood in proud array
                    beside Pante's stream,
the East-Saxon front-line
                    and the Viking army.
They could not inflict
                    any harm on each other;
death was delivered
                    by arrow's flight only.
The flood receded.
                    The pirates stood ready,
the host of the Vikings
                    eager for battle.
The hero's protector then ordered,
                    a battle-stern warrior,

Wulfstan by name,
                    to hold the causeway.
He was brave with his kinsmen,
                              this son of Ceola.
With his spear
              he laid low
him who first boldly
                    stepped on the causeway.

With Wulfstan there stood
                        two fearless warriors,
Aelfere and Maccus,
                    two of the bravest.
They refused at that ford
                        to yield in the slightest
but boldly defended
                    the attack of their foemen,
while they were still able
                          to wield their weapons.

When the Vikings perceived
                          and saw keenly
that the causeway's defenders
                              were fierce in resistance,
they turned to deception
                        and sought to be granted
for their warriors a landing
                            over the causeway.

The earl then began
                    because of his pride
to grant too much ground
                        to the hostile host.
Then Byrhtelm's son
                    began to shout out

across the cold water;
                              the warriors listened.

'Now land is laid open
                              come quickly toward us,
men to the battle.
                    God alone knows
who'll hold sway
                    on this field of battle'

Advanced then the wolves of slaughter
                                        untroubled by water,
the Viking army,
                    went west over Panta,
across the bright water,
                              bearing their bucklers,
upholding their shields,
                              the seamen went landward.
There with his warriors
                              ready for battle
Byrthnoth stood stoutly
                              against the oncoming enemy.
He ordered the shield-bearers
                                   to form the shield-hedge,
commanded his troops
                              hold fast against foe.
The fight was at hand
                              when men who were doomed
would meet their perdition.

                         Clamour rose on earth,
ravens wheeled above
                         and the carrion-keen eagle.
From their fists men let fly,
                              hurled from their hands

hard-as-file spears,

        savagely sharpened.

Bows were set busy,

        point struck buckler,

bitter the onslaught,

        warriors fell to earth,

soldiers on both sides.

        Wulfmaer was wounded,

sought death in battle,

        Byrhtnoth's kinsman,

the son of his sister,

        cruelly hacked down.

To the Vikings then

        requital was rendered.

Eadward, I heard,

        slaughtered with sword

an oncoming foeman,

        struck down at his feet

the death-doomed warrior.

        His prince proffered thanks

when the time was fitting

        for such a deed done.

Stood stoutly then

        the soldiers in battle,

keenly considered

        who first with his spear-point

could despoil of his life

        a fated enemy,

a warrior with weapons.

        Slaughter fell on earth.

His men stood resolute

                    at Byrhtnoth's urging

who bade each warrior

                    focus on battle,

ponder how he might

                    from the Danesmen win glory.

A war-hardened man

                    uplifted his shield in defence,

and advanced toward the lord:

                    each was resolute,

intent on the slaughter.

                    The seaman hurled his spear;

it wounded the earl,

                    the lord of warriors,

who struck with his shield

                    and forced back the shaft

that sprang back broken.

                    Emboldened with rage

the earl struck that Viking,

                    pierced with his lance

skilfully pointed

                    the neck of that warrior,

the sudden-raider,

                    striking him dead.

Quickly he hurled forth

                    his lance at another;

it pierced his coat-of-mail,

                    breaking it open;

its poisonous point

                    through his breast heart-wounded.

The earl rejoiced then,

                    laughed out bravely,

gave thanks up to God
                    for the deeds that day given.
But a Viking soldier
                    flung a spear from his fist;
it flew through the air
                    and struck down Byrhtnoth.
There stood by his side
                    a youthful warrior,
a young man in battle,
                    Wulfstan's son,
Wulfmaer the young.
                    Boldly he plucked out
the spear from the warrior,
                    the spear all gory,
flung it back again
                    at him who had struck his lord;
it laid him low on earth.
                    There stepped then forward
a warrior with weapons
                    who wanted the earl's rings,
the plunder of battle,
                    the decorated sword.
Byrhtnoth plucked out
                    his sword from its sheath,
broad and bright-edged,
                    and struck at the coat-of-mail.
But he was hindered
                    by one of the seafarers
who struck and wounded
                    the arm of the earl.
The gold-hilted sword
                    fell then to earth.
The earl could not hold the hard sword,
                    wield his weapon.

The grey-haired warrior
                              made address to his warriors,
bade them fare forth,
                       his valiant companions.
He could not stand firmly,
                              his feet would not serve.
Then he looked heavenward
                              and made his oration:
'To You I give thanks,
                       ruler of peoples,
for all of those joys
                  I have had in this world.
Gracious Lord,
              my sorest need now
is You grant me this goodness
                              that my soul should now journey
into Your keeping,
                   prince of the angels,
that it peacefully pass;
                         I beseech You
that the fiends of Hell
                        may not do it injury'
The heathens hewed him down
                              and both men beside him,
Aelfnoth and Wulfmaer,
                       both were laid low
close by their prince,
                       they gave up their lives.
They turned from the slaughter
                              those eager to leave.
The son of Odda
              was first to take to flight.
Godric fled the fray,
                      forsook his valiant lord

who many horses
                    had given him.
The very horse he mounted
                    was his lord's own possession
along with its trappings,
                    a deed most unjust.

His brothers fled with him,
                    both galloped away,
Godwin and Godwig,
                    not caring for battle,
hasty for flight,
                    seeking the woodland,
to hide in that fastness
                    and secure their own lives.
And many more men,
                    too shameful to mention,
forgot the rewards
                    their lord had bestowed on them.
Just so in the past
                    in the hall of assembly
Offa had told him
                    that many spoke boldly
who later in stress
                    would fail to bear up.
The prince of the people
                    had fallen,
Aethelred's earl.
                    His household troops could perceive
that their lord was laid low.

                    Then eagerly hastened
proud thanes and brave men,
                    desiring to die

or avenge their loved one.
                              The son of Aelfric,
a youthful warrior,
                        with speech urged them forward.
Aelfwine then spoke,
                        made speech out boldly:
'Remember those times
                        when we on our benches
were drinking our mead
                        and we raised up a pledge,
heroes in hall,
                        hard strife to endure.
The time is now fitting
                        to test one's bravery.
I will tell to you all
                        the line of my blood.
Descended am I
                        of a high race of Mercia.
My grandfather was Ealhhelm,
                              a noble of wisdom,
world-prosperous.
                        In front of the people
no thanes shall reproach me
                        with flight from this army
in search of my homeland,
                        my prince having fallen,
hewn down in battle,
                        it is my greatest of griefs;
he was both my kinsman and lord.'

Then he went forward
                        mindful of battle,
struck with his spear-point
                        a pirate warrior,

laid him down dead
                              slain by his weapon.
He urged on his friends,
                              his companions and comrades.
Offa brandished his spear-point,
                              spoke out loudly:

'You, Aelfwine,
                have admonished the thanes,
a thing that was needed.
                              Now our prince lies low,
the earl on the earth,
                              we must
exhort one another,
                              each warrior to battle
while he may wield weapon,
                              grip spear and good sword.
Odda's coward son, Godric,
                              betrayed his companions.
Many men thought
                it was our lord they saw
when they saw him ride off
                              on our lord's proud horse.
He divided the army
                on this field of battle,
shattered the shield-hedge.
                              Cursed be his deed
that he caused so many
                              to flee from the battle.'
Leofsunu spoke
                and raised up his shield:
'My promise I swear
                that I'll not leave here,
flee a mere footstep,
                              but onward will go

vengeance to take
                for the death of my lord.
There'll be no need in Sturmere
                    for heroes to taunt
that I lordless
          home journeyed,
turned aside from the fray;
                but a weapon shall take me,
a spear and a sword

He stepped out with wrath
                and he fought resolutely,
scorning to flee.
            Dunnere then spoke,
brandished his spear,
            this humble churl
cried out over all,
            exhorted that everyone
should take vengeance for Byrhtnoth:
                  'Intent on avenging
the prince in the battle
            no man can waver
nor mourn for life *lost.*'

The retainers went forth,
              the fierce bearers-of-shields,
careless of life,
          stoutly to battle.
To God they then prayed
             to grant them vengeance
for their dear lord's death,
           and to wreak slaughter
on their Viking foemen.
           Their hostage gave aid,

Aescferth, son of Ecglaf,

                    of noble Northumbrians,

unwavering in warfare.

                He hurled many a spear,

struck many a shield,

                  at times a man wounded

while weapons he wielded.

Eadward the tall

              still in the battle-line.

was ready and eager,

                broke out in boasting

he would not a foot's length

                    flee from the fray

nor would he retreat

                when his leader lay low.

He broke the shield-hedge,

                  fought against foemen,

until he had nobly

              avenged the death of his giver-of-treasurer

upon the bold seamen

                before he was slaughtered.

Likewise did Aetheric.

                a noble companion,

Sibyrht's brother,

             eager, impetuous,

fought *resolutely*.

              Split the embossed shield

many others also.

The brave made defence,

                broke the shield's rim.

The coat-of-mail sang

           a terrible song.

Offa struck a seaman

           while the battle raged on,

so he fell on the earth,

           kinsman of Gadd

sought the ground.

           Quick in the combat

was Offa hewn down,

           yet he had fulfilled

the promise he made his prince

           as he boasted before

to his giver-of-rings

           that they both to their stronghold

would ride safe to their homeland

           or fall at the invaders' hands

on the field of the battle,

           perished with wounds.

He lay as was fitting

           next to his prince.

There was breaking of shields,

           the seamen came onward,

enraged by the battle.

           Then Wistan went forth,

the son of Thurstan,

           fought against foemen;

in the midst of the throng

           the killer of three

until Wigelin's son

           lay low on the battle-field0.

In the hostile encounter

           the warriors stood staunchly,

resolute on conflict.
                              Fighters fell
weary with wounds;
                              slaughter fell to earth.
Oswald and Eadwold,
                              the two of them brothers,
meantime in speech
                              exhorted their kinsmen,
bade them endure
                              in the throe of their stress,
make use of their weapons
                              with full resolution.
Byrhtwold spoke out,
                              raised up his shield.
The old retainer
                              brandished his buckler,
exhorted his warriors,
                              spoke out fearlessly:
'Our resolve must be tougher,
                              the heart bolder,
courage be greater,
                              as our might lessens.
Here lies our leader
                              cut down in combat,
a good man in the dust.
                              May he ever regret
who thinks to forsake
                              and flee from this fray.
I am old and wise in life
                              and will not go from here.
By the side of my loved lord
                              it is my desire to lie.'

Then Godric,

         Aethelgar's son,

urged on the men,

            let fly his spear

into the Viking host.

             He was first of his people

to advance toward the host.

              He struck and he hewed down

until he fell in the battle.

            He was not that Godric

who fled from the fight.

Lightning Source UK Ltd.
Milton Keynes UK
UKHW040221110219
336952UK00001B/68/P